CAPE EDITIONS 32

General Editor: NATHANIEL TARN

Soap

Francis Ponge

Translated from the French by
Lane Dunlop

JONATHAN CAPE
THIRTY BEDFORD SQUARE
LONDON

First published in Great Britain 1969
by Jonathan Cape Ltd, 30 Bedford Square, London WC1
Translated from the French *Le Savon*

SBN Paperback edition 224 61659 5
Hardback edition 224 61658 7

Printed and bound in Great Britain
by Richard Clay (The Chaucer Press), Ltd
Bungay, Suffolk

BEGINNING OF THE BOOK

The reader, right off, is kindly asked (he will very soon understand why) – I mean to say: for taking off – to give himself, in his imagination, *German ears*.

And to use them now and then, each time – without my having to remind him – that we come to some verbal disturbance *meant rather to be heard*: these passages always striking his eyes as nebulosities cursively slanting towards the right (or, shall we say, since we are still circling on a path of Babel: *in italics*).

As soon as our SOAP has been put into orbit, none of this will be necessary.

SOAP

Ladies and Gentlemen,

Perhaps you are going to listen ... You have, in any case, begun to hear ... BOOM! *(Are you listening?) You are now hearing the first lines of a text, ... the reading of the German translation of a text, written originally in French ...*

Written then, not by me, the German announcer whose voice you hear ... but by the French author, who speaks to you in my voice.

He has written this.

Or rather – *if he were speaking himself – and, in reality, he is speaking to you himself, in my voice – he would say to you,* he says to you: No, I have not written *this,* I write it, *I am in the act of writing it, German listeners, for you to hear.*

I am in the act of writing these first lines. I am no more along in it than you. I am not more advanced *than you. We are going to* advance, *are* advancing *already,* together; *you hearing, me speaking; aboard the same train, or the same boat.*

*

And yet, in fact, where am I? I am seated, myself, at my table, in France, in my house. As for you, God knows where you are. You know well, yourself, where you are, you know it better than I. You also know if you are listening or only hearing, as you go about your business in your apartment and, perhaps, even, as you have some conversation … BOOM *!! From here on, I will pretend that you are listening to me …*

So listen !

*

Ladies and Gentlemen,

When it was suggested that I write some text for you, an idea came to me at once, a very selfish idea: that of profiting from this occasion to complete a work, begun many years ago, yet which I have never managed, despite numerous efforts, to come to the end of.

Thanks to you, thanks to this idea that I have, of our advancing together, I will be able, in one way or another, to succeed in doing this today.

Much obliged!

Here I am then, at my table, much obliged to write and, on the table, to my left, a dossier.

The dossier of my notes for this work, the voluminous dossier of my notes … for twenty-three years!

But wait! Achtung! Attention!

Listen to the noise of this same dossier which I have just grasped, which I am now lifting, and which I will, for you to hear, let fall again on my table …

(Noise.)

Did you hear?

Well then, now I am going to open this dossier. But first of all, what is there written on the cover of this dossier?

This, in very large handwritten characters in black ink: SOAP.

*

Soap, Ladies and Gentlemen, die Seife, die Seifenkugel, *you know, certainly,* what *it is.*

You use it every day.

You have a very definite idea of it, which we all share, and which this word suffices perfectly to represent.

It concerns a reality of the physical world.

And for me as well, of course, it is this.

But, for me, Soap, well, it is, above all, today even more so, *this dossier, this precious dossier!*

Ah! this dossier-soap, *this soap*-dossier, *what trouble, for twenty or twenty-five years, it has given me, this* soap! *which I am going to rid myself of today, in a few minutes (what luck!).*

Let's begin! Let's open the dossier!

*

But first, I must warn you!

You will be startled, perhaps – as it is not very usual in literature – by the frequent, the tedious repetitions which the present text contains.

Very often you will remark: 'But he repeats himself! But I have already heard that, just a few minutes ago!'

Well then, should I apologize for this? No! I do not overly like to apologize and then, after all, these ways and manners which you readily admit, is it not so, in matters of music: these repetitions, these renewals da capo, *these variations on the same theme, these compositions in the fugue form which you readily admit in music, which you admit and enjoy – why should they, in literature, be forbidden?*

Can you tell me why?

In any case, you have been warned.

This is how, after all, I work, this is how developments happen in me, this is how the mind goes forward, – and it is very necessary, isn't it? to be honest, very necessary not to tamper with the mind's movement?

Ladies and Gentlemen, here are the first notes, then, which I put down on paper in April 1942, *at Roanne, a small town in central France, where my family and I were, as the phrase was,* in retreat *– or* refugees.

There we were, then, in the midst of war, that is to say of restrictions *of all kinds, and soap, real soap, was particularly missed. We had only the worst* ersätze *– which did not* froth *at all.*

Could this have been one of the unconscious causes for what I have to call my inspiration *of soap, in April* 1942 *… ?*

But here are the first notes – and from here on, I will not stop again …

No more commentaries …

SOAP, *only soap!*

SOAP

Roanne, April 1942

If I rub my hands with it, soap foams, exults …
The more complaisant it makes them, supple,
smooth, docile, the more it slobbers, the more
its rage becomes voluminous, pearly …
Magic stone!
The more it forms with air and water
clusters of scented grapes,
explosive …
Water, air and soap
overlap, play
at leapfrog, form
combinations less chemical than
physical, gymnastical, acrobatical …
Rhetorical?

There is much to say about soap. Precisely everything that it tells about itself until the complete disappearance, the exhaustion of the subject. This is precisely the object suited to me.

*

Soap has much to say. May it say it with volubility, enthusiasm. When it has finished saying it, it no longer is.

*

A sort of stone, but which does not let itself be rolled around in nature: it slips between your fingers, and melts before your eyes rather than be rolled about by water.

The game exactly consists, then, of holding it in your fingers and chafing it with the right dose of water, so as to obtain from it a voluminous, pearly reaction ...

If one lets it remain in the water, on the contrary, it perishes in confusion.

*

A sort of stone, but (*yes! a-sort-of-stone-but*) which does not let itself be unilaterally caressed by the forces of nature: it slips between their fingers, melts before their eyes.

It melts before the eyes, rather than let itself be rolled about by water.

*

There is, in nature, nothing comparable to soap. No pebble (quoit), no stone so slippery, whose reaction in your fingers, if you have managed to hold it there while chafing it with the right dose of water, is such a voluminous, pearly slobber, consisting of so many clusters of plethoric bubbles.

The hollow grapes, the scented grapes of soap.

Agglomerations.

It gobbles the air, it gobbles the water all over your fingers.

Although at first it reposes, inert and amorphous

in a saucer, the power is in the hands of soap to make our own willing, complaisant to use water, to abuse water in its least details.

So we slip from words to meanings with a lucid inebriety, or rather an effervescence, an iridescent though lucid and cold ebullition, which we come out of with hands purer than before this exercise began.

*

Soap is a sort of stone, but not natural: sensitive, susceptible, complicated.

It has a particular sort of dignity.

Far from taking pleasure (or at least passing its time) in being rolled about by the forces of nature, it slips between their fingers; it melts before the eyes, rather than let itself be unilaterally rolled about by water.

At this point, the circumstances of the period obliged us to leave Roanne and, when the next section was written, I was in Coligny, a village north of Lyon.

Coligny, June 3rd, 1943

There is nothing in nature like soap. No stone so slippery, whose reaction in your fingers – if you have managed to hold it there while chafing it with water – is such a voluminous, pearly slobber, consisting of so many clusters of such plethoric bubbles.

In the shape of hollow and artificially scented grapes, soap gobbles the water, gobbles the air all over your fingers, encloses much air by its way of enlacing, embracing, spheres, circumlocutions, vicious circles, iridescent, of a waterlily-like body, a curiously elastic flesh of nymph.

Bombast, enthusiasm, volubility.

The iridescent though extra-lucid and cold ebullition ...

Yes. Quite amorphous, at first, as it reposes in a saucer, the power is in the hands of soap to make our own complaisant to use, to abuse water in its least details, to make it attached to us, solicitous, attentive, to transform it so that it henceforth wants to dance with us for ever in its veils, its robes, its ballroom sashes. And, on our part, we exhaust it to the last degree. ... You really feel that there is something vicious in this, a sort of mutual abuse.

(Nothing is more like a kneading trough than a washbowl, yet it is a kneading trough in which man never finds anything but his hands.)

... So we slip from words to meanings ... by a lucid and glistening inebriety, or rather an effervescence, a cold ebullescence which, besides, we come out of, and here is the great lesson – with cleaner, purer hands than before this exercise began.

*

Soap was made by man for his body's use; yet it does not willingly attend him. This inert stone is nearly as hard to hold as a fish. See it slip from me and like a frog dive into the basin again ... emitting also at its own expense a blue cloud of evanescence, of confusion ...

What a magnificent way of life soap shows us!

In the sun its forehead dries, darkens, hardens, wrinkles, cracks. Cares split it. Yet it never conserves itself so well as when thus inactive, forgotten.

In water, on the contrary, where it becomes supple, circulates, seems at ease – one has difficulty recovering it – where it moves around, grows agile, then voluble, eloquent, – it spends itself at a disquieting rate, it does not remain uninconvenienced ... Is this what is called leading a dissipated life ... ? I see in it as well the sign of a particular dignity ...

*

For a piece of soap, the principal virtues are enthusiasm and volubility. At any rate ease of elocution.

This, which is excessively simple, has none the less never been said. Even by the specialist in commercial publicity. And how much do the soap-manufacturers offer me? – Not a penny! They have never even thought of it! Yet soap and I will show them what we can do …

*

There is something adorable in the personality of soap. Why adorable? Because its behaviour is at once in the highest degree appealing and completely inimitable.

Here is a sort of mediocre pebble, flatly reposing in the plainest saucer (sometimes the most damaged) in the house.

A man comes with dirty hands. Then the forgotten soap gives itself up to him. Not without some coquetry. It swathes itself in glistening, iridescent veils and, at the same time, tends to vanish, to flee. No more fugitive stone in nature. But then, the game exactly consists of holding it in the fingers and chafing it, by the addition of a dose of water sufficient to obtain a voluminous, pearly slobber, whereas if one left it to remain in the water, it would perish in confusion.

For soap has its particular dignity. It is a stone, but one which does not allow itself to be unilaterally rolled about by the forces of nature. It slips between their fingers, clings to some part of the bottom and melts before the eyes, rather than let itself be unilaterally caressed by water.

Man abuses it. If he rubs his hands with it, soap foams, exults. The more it rages, the more voluminous and pearly its slobber becomes, the more complaisant it makes his hands, supple, smooth, docile.

Magic stone!

... The more it forms, with air and water, clusters of scented grapes, explosive.

Water, air and soap overlap, then, play at leapfrog, form bombastic and slight combinations which a breath, a smile, the least interior vanity, the slightest exaggeration cause to explode ...

Or a catastrophe of water.

One feels that I have exaggerated the developments, the variations; that there is something soapy, slobbering, foamy in the style – like the froth in the nostrils of a galloping horse –

Be sure that I have done so on purpose.

Knowing that a paragraph of pure reason (or irony?) would suffice to cleanse, dissolve and rinse all this.

(This version, called 'soap-gibberish', is dated June 3rd, 1943 at Coligny.)

*

Coligny, June 9th, 1943

There is nothing in nature comparable to soap. No stone is so modest nor, at the same time, so magnificent.

To be frank, there is something adorable about its personality. Its behaviour is inimitable.

It begins with a perfect reserve.

Soap displays at first a perfect self-control, though more or less discreetly scented. Then, as soon as one occupies oneself with it, I won't say what fire, of course, but what magnificent elan! What utter enthusiasm in the gift of itself! What generosity! What volubility, almost inexhaustible, unimaginable!

One may, besides, soon be done with it, yet this adventure, this brief encounter leaves you – this is what is sublime – with hands as clean as you've ever had.

*

Because of this object's qualities I must expatiate a little, make it froth before your eyes.

SOAP

Coligny, June 1943

ABSTRACT THEME

(Idea of The Intellectual Toilet)

If I wished to prove that purity is not obtained by silence, but by any exercise of language (in certain conditions, a certain ridiculous little object held in the hands), followed by a sudden catastrophe of pure water,

Would anything be better than soap?

*

Violent desire to wash one's hands.

Dear reader, I suppose that you sometimes want to wash your hands!

For your intellectual toilet, reader, here is a text on soap.

*

Coligny, June 1943

... Here then, dear reader, for your intellectual toilet (if you are one of my friends, you will feel an imperious need for it at times), here is a little piece of *real soap*.

It is a fact that man cannot clean himself with simple water, even if he stood under drenching torrents, nor in a fresh wind, however scented, nor by silence, nor by prayer (even waist deep in the Jordan), nor by suicide in the darkest source (despite all sorts of prejudices current on this head).

It is necessary – and it is enough, but necessary – to have in hand (in the mouth) something more material and perhaps less natural, something artificial and voluble, something which displays itself, develops, and which loses itself, uses itself up at the same time. Something which is very much like speech employed in certain conditions ...

... In a word: *a little piece of soap.*

This sky-blue nut of mist is necessary. This cloud of very fragile spheres.

This prestigious* (prestidigitious) stage scene behind which memory disappears.

The memory of all dirtiness dissolves and the worst solution, certainly, in this matter, is being led by your *idée fixe*, or that of your parents, to let yourself get soaked, arms folded, in some dull tributary of the Dead Sea.

Fresh start! Clean sweep!

*

Coligny, July 1943

This egg, this flat
dab, – this little
almond, which
grows so quickly
(almost instantly)

* Translator's note: I have used this word in a slightly French sense (deceptive glamour) to save the pun.

into a Chinese fish
With its veils and kimonos
and wide sleeves
Thus it celebrates its marriage
with water. Such is the gown of its marriage with
water.

*

One would never be through,
with soap!
... Yet it is necessary to return it to its saucer, to its strict appearance, its austere oval, its dry patience, and its power to serve again.

*

Coligny, July 6th, 1943

THEME (dry and modest in its saucer) AND VARIATIONS (voluminous and pearly) on SOAP (followed by a paragraph of rinsing with simple water).

For the intellectual toilet, a little piece of soap, well-handled, is enough. Where torrents of simple water would clean nothing.

Nor silence, nor your suicide in the darkest source, o absolute young man.

*

Eh: Yes! Living under the pump is good for nothing. Or even remaining in the waters of the Jordan.

(The simplest washbowl would be much better ...) Unless one holds in one's hand (and uses it) this mediocre pebble (of magical nature) ... unless one gives it speech.

Scarcely has one solicited it, than what eloquence!

What enthusiasm, what glistening volubility does it not lavish on the hands that deliver it from its mutism, then on the whole body of its liberator.

What exultation, which it is very necessary that we take into account!

Perhaps you have already understood me, so that I might stop here. But what! The very nature of my subject authorizes me to enjoy myself, and to make you enjoy more voluminous yet slight developments and (as they should be) ephemeral and purificatory.

*

Coligny, July 8th, 1943

SOAP

Thank God, a certain gibberish is called for concerning soap, touching soap. There is more to be gibbered than said, touching soap. And it is not necessary to disquiet oneself, to disquiet oneself about always saying the same thing. One may, one should gibber. To gibber, is to say what? To make oneself a little ridiculous, to ridicule words a little. But always with soap in hand. Then, placing it again in its saucer, to interrupt the exercise with a catastrophe of simple water (a turn of the faucet, a paragraph is enough).

And the marvellous thing is, that one comes out of it with cleaner hands, purer hands.

*

Let us go further, and say that for any kind of serious cleaning, a piece of soap is necessary; let us say that is enough.

It is known, in fact, that one cannot clean oneself properly with simple water. Even if one stood under the purest torrents. Or in the silence of the darkest and coldest source, where the temptation might occur to you, o absolute young man, of drowning yourself. Even if one dived down the well of truth, no! None of this is enough to make the dirt on the skin so much as raise its eyebrows. Thus, living under the pump is good for nothing, with the risk of hiccupping your way from life to death. And I will only cite for the sake of completeness the most obsolete solution, which is to immerse oneself up to the waist, arms folded, in some dull tributary of the Dead Sea (in water that flows towards the Dead Sea) burbling some prayer-bubbles, while touching with two moistened fingers one's forehead, navel and nipples.

Speak to me rather of the smallest washbowl, the least scrap of soap!

*

There is much to say about soap. Precisely everything that it tells about itself, when one chafes it with water in a certain way. It also looks as if it had much to say. May it say it, then. With volubility, with enthusiasm. Until the disappearance by exhaustion of its own theme. When it has finished saying it, it no longer is. The longer it is in saying it, the more it can say it at length, the more slowly it melts, the better quality it is.

Naturally, it is always saying the same thing. And it says it to no matter whom. It expresses itself in the same way to everyone.

Slobbering stone ...

That there is much, almost infinitely much, to be said about soap, is the very evidence. And perhaps to be gibbered rather than said. A certain extreme volubility is called for here. And a certain enthusiasm in wearing oneself out, giving oneself up.

May it no longer hesitate to always say the same things. And to always say them in the same way. And to say them in the same way to anyone – with exultation, it's understood. But the marvellous thing is, that one comes out of these exercises with purer hands. This is the great lesson.

And that this exercise is the most suited to intellectual hygiene, is also understood.

*

PRELUDE TO SOAP

For the toilet of the mind, a little piece of soap. Well-handled is enough. Where torrents of simple water would clean nothing. Nor silence. Nor your suicide in the darkest source, o absolute reader.

Living under the pump is good for nothing. Except

hiccups. And the triumph of the absurd, in this case, is it not to stand waist-deep in water that flees towards the Dead Sea, arms folded.

Believe me, the smallest bowl would be better ... But look at him, now, under the faucet, gushing with impatience to loosen the dry tongue of the soap.

The text immediately preceding this, recited slowly, that is to say, as carefully as it was written, seemed to me sufficiently complete to send to my two best friends at that time, Albert Camus and Jean Paulhan.

From Paulhan, no answer. But from Camus, I soon received this:

*

Extract from a letter of Albert Camus:

'As for *soap*, your intentions escape me slightly, whereas usually they are *very clear* to me. There may be an excessive ellipse; I don't really understand. Perhaps, without sacrificing anything essential, you might supple the hinges a little, oil the conjunctions. Nevertheless, the text is not to be changed. But you see it more clearly than I do. This raises a great problem, besides. To my mind, control is not achieved without an occasional abandon. Your abandon has generally been irony. Yet irony is an ellipse also. And it is for this reason that the reading of your texts gives the reader the impression that one has violated his sensibility, escarped his intelligence, that one was right to. "One", it's you.

'But the *Twelve Little Writings* allowed me to see in you a very different abandon, which I would like to see reappear now and then (this is why I like above all *The Stone* or your pieces on trees). Of course, I say "now and then", because the essential of your art is not that. It is that which you choose to do, and which you do to perfection.'

*

The silence of Paulhan, the reserve of Camus gave me much to think about, and I gradually came to conceive, so as to make my intentions clearer, as clear as possible, yet changing nothing *in the text which was to my satisfaction, adding* nothing, *not the least phrase, not the least word, of a sort of distribution of the elements of this text, by which I mean the various propositions (in the grammatical sense) of which it was made up.*

A sort of distribution, in the sense that a stage-manager (what you others call the director) *distributes the* text, *which he has the job of making a* play, *among separate voices, separate characters.*

I insist on the fact that my text *itself was to be in no way modified. It was only a question of staging.*

And here is what I ended with, by the beginning of summer 1944.

Camus, who was much engaged in theatre then, and whom I had informed of my intentions by correspondence (as he was then in Paris where he helped, for example, in the staging and private performance of Picasso's The Devil Caught By the Tail), *urged me to get this little Soap play ready. But I did not have the leisure, when I had finished it, in the state in which France found itself then (the beginning of summer* 1944), *to send it to him.*

Here, then, is what I ended with, for myself alone:

SOAP

PRELUDE
in
SAYNÈTE[1]
or
MOMON[2]

1. Contrary to what one might think, a *saynète,* much less than a little scene, is a little piece of fat, a dainty piece, at once dainty and nourishing, and even hot. Its origin is *sain,* fat, which is the *sain* in our *saindoux,** and consequently, in Spanish, *sainete*: an interlude and, in French, a little farcical skit of Spanish theatre.

2. A *momon* is a masquerade, a sort of dance done by masked figures, ending with a challenge delivered by them. Its radical is the same as in mummery. One ought to be able to so name, by extension, any work of art including its own caricature, or one in which the author was to ridicule his means of expression. The *Waltz* of Ravel is a *momon*. The genre is peculiar to periods in which rhetoric, dying, examines itself.

*

* Translator's note: lard.

Characters:

FIRST CHIMNEYSWEEP
SECOND CHIMNEYSWEEP
LITTLE CHIMNEYSWEEP (DOESN'T SPEAK)
TYPIST
THE ABSOLUTE READER
THE ABBÉ JEAN-BAPTISTE GRIBOUILLE
FIRST PHILOSOPHER
SECOND PHILOSOPHER
THE POET

The scene represents a courtyard adjacent to the park of a large house. In it there is a pool, or fairly deep spring, with dark water, flowing in a stream into the park.

Beneath a corbel in the wall of the house, on ground-floor level, a washstand: a faucet, a bowl, a saucer with a piece of soap, A Turkish towel. A pump is near by. An iron table.

In the foreground, a sloping lawn, with scattered rocks. On the rock nearest the spectator, to the right, a typewriter.

It is warm and stormy. Dust.

As the curtain rises, the chimneysweeps (two men and a small boy) are leaving the house. They make gestures to brush off the soot that coats them, passing their hands over their faces in a listless way. But evidently satisfied with the work they have just done. Looking up at the roofs and chimneys. Happy also to be through.

At the same time a group seated on the rocks or the lawn begins to break up. It comprises the Poet, the Absolute Reader, the two Philosophers and the Abbé

Jean-Baptiste Gribouille. Each holds a book or papers. It is clear that they have just been discussing something, and their gestures resemble those of the chimneysweeps. They shake themselves, adjust their clothing, smoothe their hair or beard, but their faces suggest discontent rather than fatigue. They walk back and forth behind the typist, sitting near a rock in front of her typewriter, which she has just covered again in its black oil-cloth. They bend over the sheets that have just been taken out with a dissatisfied air and, after a while, agree to have the typist destroy them. The Poet, in getting up, had left his papers behind. The Reader, more abruptly, had thrown down his book and gone towards the spring to bend over it with a sombre air.

Meanwhile, the chimneysweeps have been approaching the washstand. The poet follows them with his eye. Suddenly, he goes towards them, reaches the stand before them and, grabbing one of the pieces of soap, turns towards the others (and the public), and in a tone of voice at once inspired and questioning (and mocking) says:

THE POET. For the toilet of the mind, a little piece of soap? …

FIRST CHIMNEYSWEEP. Well handled is enough …

(The young CHIMNEYSWEEP *is already under the pump, working it.)*

FIRST PHILOSOPHER (*pointing to the small boy*). Where torrents of simple water …

SECOND CHIMNEYSWEEP (*chasing the small boy*). Would clean nothing …

THE ABSOLUTE READER (*bent over the spring*). Nor silence ...

SECOND PHILOSOPHER. Nor your suicide in the darkest source, o Absolute Reader!

(*Thunder.*

The ABBÉ JEAN-BAPTISTE GRIBOUILLE *seems seized by an holy illumination. He points to the sky with a prophetic finger, takes a statuette of Saint-Sulpice from his soutane, sets it on the table, adores it, crosses himself several times and goes to kneel beneath the pump, his hands clasped. No water comes out of the pump.*

The sun shines.)

FIRST CHIMNEYSWEEP. Living under the pump is good for nothing ...

(*The* ABBÉ *says something inaudibly.*)

SECOND CHIMNEYSWEEP. Except hiccups.

(*The* ABBÉ *raises his head, sees that there is no water, yet he has lost none of his assurance: he walks slowly, almost like a somnambulist, towards the spring, in which he immerses himself up to the waist, arms folded on his chest, gazing at the sky, as if for the Baptism in the Jordan. He will remain in this pose until the end of the act.*)

FIRST PHILOSOPHER. The triumph of the absurd, in this case, is it not ...

SECOND PHILOSOPHER. To stand waist-deep ...

FIRST PHILOSOPHER. Arms folded!

SECOND PHILOSOPHER. In water that flees towards the Dead Sea ...

SECOND CHIMNEYSWEEP. Believe me, the smallest bowl would be better ...

(*The young* BOY *has turned on the faucet, which has already filled the bowl.*)

FIRST PHILOSOPHER (*to the Poet*). But look at him, now, under the faucet gushing with impatience ...

SECOND PHILOSOPHER. To loosen the dry tongue of the soap.

THE ABSOLUTE READER (*brusquely, pointing to the statuette on the iron table*). Remove this God! Bring the table and bowl here!

(*The* CHIMNEYSWEEPS *place the table in the foreground, take away the statuette, replacing it with a bowl full of water and the saucer with its piece of soap. To the* POET:)

Let the soap speak!

(*The* POET *comes forward, takes the piece of soap and prepares to declaim while washing his hands. The* CHIMNEYSWEEPS, *having returned to the background, are by the pump, taking off their jackets. During the entire declamation they will be soaping their bare torsos under the pump with a big piece of very frothy soap, washing the little boy as well. The* TYPIST *removes the covering from her machine and, as the* POET *is about to speak, sheds her dress in a single movement, appearing naked* (or *in a bathing suit*). *The* ABSOLUTE READER *leaves the railing of the spring and goes to stand behind the* TYPIST *to follow the declamation as she blackens the sheets with it. The* PHILOSOPHERS *are seated or leaning on their elbows, listening.*

The ABBÉ *will remain motionless in the spring, in his attitude of expectant prayer ...*)

End of the PRELUDE

During the declamation which is about to follow, there will be background music, low, not at all lively but severe, rigorously contrapuntal, inspired by the sound of typewriters. In fact, this will continue throughout. At times there will also be a noise like a book's page being turned ...

From the back of the theatre a very bright projected ray of light, illuminating from floor to ceiling, will then throw the shadow of the typewriter's roller on to a screen that will replace the backdrop. On this screen, which will seem the projection of the sheet in the typewriter's roller, the text of the poem, as it is declaimed, will appear cinematically.

It's then that the declamation of the poem proper, of which I will give you an idea in a minute, would begin, and at the end of which would occur the brief final scene:

CODA
in
DIALOGUE

THE POET (*ending his declamation*). ... One would never be through with soap. Yet it is necessary to return it to its austere oval, and its power to serve again.

(*He puts the piece of soap in its saucer.*)

THE PHILOSOPHERS (*in chorus*). If he had wished to prove that purity is not obtained by silence, but by any exercise of language (in certain conditions), followed by a sudden catastrophe of fresh water, he would not have argued otherwise.

THE ABBÉ J.-B. GRIBOUILLE (*remaining waist deep in the*

spring, when the PHILOSOPHERS *say the word 'argued', he says in chorus with them, in the same tone of voice:)* Prophesied ...

(then makes the sign of the cross, but doubtless the waters of the Jordan are dirty because, touching his forehead, he leaves a black spot there.)

THE CHIMNEYSWEEPS *(in chorus) (they are white and bright, thoroughly clean, radiant and, at the same time as the* PHILOSOPHERS' *'argued' and the* ABBÉ'S *'prophesied', say:)* Was anything better than soap?

(Before the curtain starts to fall, THE POET *approaches the* ABSOLUTE READER *who, always behind the* TYPIST, *has been snatching the sheets out of the typewriter and reading them close to his eyes, – takes his arm and leads him towards the exit, saying:)*

THE POET. But if I had failed, would you perhaps find that I had stained you with ink instead?

CURTAIN

This play was never performed. I had done it, as I've said, for myself alone.

Yet, at the same time, I experienced a kind of remorse, a kind of bad conscience.

I told myself that it was beneath a writer of my type *to be satisfied with such facilities, with such expedients, in making myself understood.*

And that, in the end, a text should stand on its own and not need to be performed.

I wrote, then, a sort of short prose piece summing up the whole poem, from start to finish, so that it would, at least, constitute not a play but a book.

Here is that résumé, which I entitled THEME OF SOAP *and which was written on July 8th,* 1944.

THEME OF SOAP

... And now, dear reader, for your intellectual toilet, here is a little piece of soap. Well handled, we guarantee it will be enough. Let us hold this magic stone.

*

There is something adorable in the personality, the character of soap; something inimitable in its behaviour.

At first a reserve, a bearing, a patience in its saucer as perfect as those of the pebble stone. But, at the same time, less roughness, less dryness. It is, certainly, obstinate, compact, self-disciplined, holding itself in check, but also amenable, attractive, polished, soft, agreeable in the hands. And scented (although not *sui generis*). More vulgar, perhaps, but in compensation more sociable.

This is due to the oil of which it is made and which is the basis of its qualities. No bark, or even skin: since it makes no claim to be autonomous.

Whereas the stone is more than misanthropic: it seems to ignore man altogether, – soap is made for man, and does not forget him; it in no way forgets its duty.

It is a stone which did not exist in nature. It slips

through it with a perfect ease, grace, amiability and nimbleness.

*

This would not be much in itself, though already it concerns very valuable qualities. But let's observe in it others, even more touching.

Let us watch it in a watery surrounding. It immediately shows, there, a kind of shy agitation. It circulates, flees, makes a thousand affected gestures, swathes itself in veils and finally prefers to dissolve, give up the ghost, to give up the body rather than let itself be caressed, unilaterally rolled about by water.

Shall we say that it leads a dissipated life there? Doubtless ... But this may also be understood as a particular kind of dignity.

Besides, the water is very moved and troubled by it, very seriously punished. It does not easily rid itself of the traces of its crime. Does not manage to rid itself of them except by a considerable afflux of re-inforcements, except by calling on quantity.

At this point, let's take the soap out of the water and consider each of the two adversaries. One, very much diminished, attenuated, but not in its quality. The other, an enormous amount troubled, having lost face. Which one is the victor?

*

But let us continue and we will arrive at the raison d'être, the destination (or destiny) of soap. Let the trio form. Let a man enter. A man with dirty hands. A man who has need of soap. Who recognizes its qualities, properties, susceptibilities, its faults and knows how to make them serve him, to use them and flatter them, to make the most of them.

Then, one witnesses a marvellous elan of generosity, enthusiasm, the exultation of our object in the gift of itself.

It reveals itself, at last, according to its genius. Its volubility. This is its happy hour, its hap. It gives itself utterly, exults, gibbers, etc. Its caresses, embraces, manifestations, seem to have no end.

It happens, then, that one abuses it. Aesthetic perfection. Bubbles ...

*

Nevertheless, it is necessary to end, to set a limit to (to rein in) these elans. A paragraph of simple water will be enough. And you will perceive, then, that the exercise of soap will have left you cleaner, purer and sweeter smelling than you were before. That it has changed you for the better, re-qualified you.

As for itself, it returns to its austere oval, at once austere and attractive. It retracts itself and waits to be mobilized again. Resumes its modest attitude, its taciturn air. Goes back to its patience, its serenity.

Let us pass rapidly over the four or five periods that followed: the winter of 1944, the whole of 1945, the first half of 1946 – during which time I had many other things to do and no longer occupied myself with Soap.

However, in the summer of 1946, when we returned to spend our vacation at Coligny, I had the leisure to work on it again. One will note that circumstances had changed by then – and for myself as well, for me personally.

Many essays on my work, after that of Sartre's, had been published. And I was, besides, although still sincerely communist, about to leave the Party of that name, the directives of which, in matters I was competent to judge, I no longer agreed with. All this is evident in the fragments below.

Coligny, July 17th–22nd, 1946

'FRANCIS PONGE, or *the happy man*': so I have heard myself called.

Certainly: very happy with all that is happening to me and, particularly, to have (as it happened) had the time to observe with some attention a little piece of soap.

If you have a few minutes to spare, and if it pleases you to bear with me again ...

But wait: let's begin at the beginning. And crumple, first, then throw away every rough draft imprinted with ordinary bad taste on the wrappers of the object.

Let's grasp it, naked as it is.

*

If it has happened (as it does happen) that my mind has exercised itself to best advantage with the simplest things, of the slightest reputation, and even with the most derided, I hope that this will not be held against me. Certainly, far from deriving the least pride from it, I accuse myself for it and immediately place myself far below those of my fellow artists who deal with serious or moving objects. If I momentarily lose my head at times, so as to begin to believe those benevolent critics who praise to the sky, if not my successes, at least the ambitions they credit me with, please believe that I very quickly come to earth again.

As a consolation I tell myself that several French artists, and not the least ones, may have been in my situation : La Fontaine and Rameau were among them. And Chardin and now Braque.

Yet it may be that some experience (repeated several times) would lead me to suppose, if I felt the need of a slightly pretentious justification, that such application of the mind, if not praiseworthy, might at least appear natural in such an age as we are fated to live in.

Is it necessary to mention the disagreeable (to say the least) events or spectacles which we have been obliged to endure since coming into this world? I have scruples in doing so. Although, to be truthful, I think that no other age can have witnessed any which were more terrible, more trying of sensibility.

....

(Develop this a little)

....

But, perhaps, to consider it closely, all this is no more serious than a simple illness, – or simply the awareness of the human condition.

More spectacular, even, it may be! I will not decide.

At any rate society everywhere – and each individual – have shown themselves to be bewildered, thrown into despair and aberration. And it has become plain that self-control, sang-froid, patience and equanimity in themselves were not enough to put the mind to rights again, or console the spirit.

At the same time, i.e. our time, the consciousness of human responsibility and guilt – wrongly or rightly – has become extremely developed. And, whether this is right or wrong, I find it very admirable and very touching.

Whence an equally trying moral despair, a remorse and a resolution (followed by disillusion, etc.).

So much so that the lessons of the classic sages have seemed inadequate and, strictly speaking, inapplicable to the modern mentality. How could a man troubled by such feelings be satisfied with the advice of Socrates, Aristotle, Montaigne or Pascal, Voltaire or Vauvenargues? I am aware that many have sought refuge in them. I am afraid that this has been to the detriment of a certain integrity.

For my part, then, I will not foolhardily advise men to rely each on themselves, to search for tranquillity as the only good to be wished for etc.* I would truly have scruples in doing so, mainly because I want to be able to be read by the members of an unhappy, unfortunate class, whose first duty I figure *it* to be to rise, by strength and courage, to a materially better situation. And I think also that such persons and such classes, having had the luck to find recently a doctrine which exalts them and a party which puts them in the way to victory, would be very wrong to turn away from these to who knows what ancient theories of

* Translator's note: It should be noted that when Ponge says 'etc.' he is often referring to, often quoting exactly from, some passage in earlier work. Here, for example, it is 'The Employee's Monologue' (*Twelve Little Writings*, 1926).

resignation and stoicism, which I am aware of as favouring their exploiters.

And as for these exploiters, how could an artist like them when he sees them, insensitive to good and to qualities of taste, of delicacy and wit, causing their predecessors (aristocratic) in human exploitation to be regretted? How can he not wish for their defeat and their replacement by that oppressed class, which most likely possesses in itself the resources of fervour and purity proper to the birth of what is beautiful and delicate, which is the supreme good that I wish for men.

Thus I would turn no one away from the duty of action and revolt. On the contrary, when the situation is pregnant (and, in a way of speaking, it always is), considering that each man (even an artist) must allot a part at least of his activity to civic action, I would take the part of the side I have mentioned.

Be that as it may, it would not be honest on my part (besides, it would do no good and even be harmful) to renounce in any way the values which a formation, no doubt bourgeois, but finally human as well, has made me consider once and for all as the worthiest of being sought or defended (so much so that if I wish for the revolution, – or that historical movement which will bring the class now being exploited to power – it is in the hope that the greatest number of people – and, in the end, all human beings – will be placed in the condition one day of being able to seek these values, to establish them and to enjoy them). What are these values? I have just said: the beautiful and the delicate.

Two consequences for my own conduct will stem

from this. First of all, within that one party which I have in the past accepted, I will agitate – while recognizing, as I said before, that it is wholly qualified to lead my friends and myself on the paths of victory – and that a party of crude, wretched little people would not know how to accept ways which do not suit them – I will agitate, then, for the conservation (either on the sidelines or on the sly) of the noble, delicate values to which I give the highest place, as being the aim of life. I am persuaded that one could not with impunity trample on those very values for which, after all, one is fighting.

Other considerations, besides, militate in favour of this thesis. Notably, the consideration of those psychological characteristics which are unanimously agreed to be French (etc. ... *to be developed:* taste for truth, irrespect of persons, realism and spiritual courage: Rabelais, Boileau, Montaigne, Molière, Voltaire, etc.).

*

Since, to begin, it is always necessary to break something, even if this should only be silence, let's break open, then, crumple and throw away every note or rough draft imprinted with ordinary false taste on the wrappers of the object ... Let's grasp it, naked as it is.

And first of all, since it presents itself stripped in two principal forms: the cube (or parallelepiped), or in ovoid form, let us note à propos of these two forms that one tends towards the other; the first not lasting well (if more convenient for packing, placing and sending in boxes, cases and trucks), the least usage making it start at once to tend gradually towards the second. The latter, on the contrary, conserves itself, slowly perfects itself in its very erosion.

It is, besides, the predestined form of our object (this ovoid form): because it has the virtues of flight, of *success,* that is of leaving the hands when it has finished being useful.

*

If, as one of my critics has revealed – making waves like none other in his little bathtub – if then, 'any word about any object is too much', well, I am sorry to tell him that this doesn't apply where soap is concerned.

And this is why, doubtless, at this time, I have chosen this subject. Because it was necessary to find that one – and perhaps the only one – which reassures me, which justifies speech – and even stammering, gibberish … Now, there is evidently much to be said about soap. Not, of course, to the point of making our hands puffy, like certain children bent on forming bubbles … nor causing them to resemble chicken giblets … Yet observe, at the first contact, this prestidigitation, these sleights of hand …

This is said to tempt you.

Nevertheless, at first, as our subject requires, we will remain dry and boring for a few paragraphs …

*

Coligny, July 25th, 1946

WITH SOAP IN THE BATHTUB OF GNOTHI SEAUTON

SOAP? Yes, here I am, soapy with it; the water is saturated with it ...

I amused myself a little too much, I must admit, with soap in the bathtub of Gnothi Seauton, perhaps at the risk of a puffy skin ...

I amused myself for a long time; to be truthful, amused and bored myself (perversely), like a child lazy in washing himself in his bathtub, in making this soap froth.

Today, I am slightly ashamed of this. I see it with a rinsed eye. I would not want to impose on you with all this ... Perhaps it is not worth the trouble. We shall be done with it soon enough ...

It must not be given, in my work, more place or time than it occupies in the day, or life, of a man of my condition ... A rather important place, to be truthful, among the clean young bourgeoisie ...

*

Coligny, August 2nd, 1946

Absurd, perhaps, yet I have decided to destroy my notes for SOAP on August 15th.

At that time, the definitive text must not only be written, but I must know it by heart (since I have decided to destroy *everything*).

... Or that I know my notes by heart then; and it will have been necessary to make them such as may be recited (and first of all learnt).

But anything – you will say – can be recited by heart! All that's needed is application.

Exactly, dear friends; it is this application that I am seeking. It is to some application that I seek to bring myself. And to bring you at the same time.

Be sure, soap is only a pretext.

Could you have ever thought otherwise?

I only require of you that you recite my own words with me.

That I force you to accompany me at my own pace.

And I would very much like, in addition, of course, for this pace to charm you. And, firstly, that it charm me. But haven't you already deserted me? There, there! We will go more slowly; for we have started out much too fast ...

*

You tell me that I am using up the credit which one allowed me for my previous work. That these preliminary ramblings are without any interest, and that I would not have found it necessary to begin a poem in this way when my name was unknown.

'Why not get to the heart of the matter, and startle the reader by the brusque apparition of a naked, concrete form, as it is in your particular power to do?

'Dear friend, you disappoint us.'

*

Because it is very necessary that we admit the evidence (and that you, reader, make of it what you can): it is towards objects known as the simplest, the least important, even the most ridiculous, that the play of my mind is exercised to best advantage, because then and then alone does it seem possible for it to make use of its particular ideas in their particular form. [It seems to me legitimate and useful, even necessary (and agreeable as well) to publish my particular ideas or opinions in their particular form.] – Finally, to express my mind, because then and then alone do these ideas, these opinions seem ineluctable, revelatory to it, and *transport it,* transport it to their expression from which, besides, they are in no way distinguishable ... From the moment, then, that I have realized this, I have, *primo,* neither to glorify myself nor beat my breast, to reproach myself nor justify myself: it is a question of fact, a piece of good luck and I give it as such and I give it *to myself* as such (I assume it); *secundo* certain subjects, at the same time, impose themselves on me – and among them, for example, soap foremost – such as my critics will kindly note, – I do not *look* for anything more in them than what I find, I do not *attempt* anything, I have no secondary intention or ambition and, above all, no concern with philosophy (that attic, that sordid bed): in our house there is ease, order, it shines. Là, tout n'est qu'ordre, beauté, luxe, calme et volupté. And, finally, even the bourgeoisie. And I would be angry with myself for showing anything but what I am capable of putting in order, of making attractive and comfortable, of polishing, of making gleam and of opening, at last, to the beams of smiling sensuousness.

*

Reader, you will have to do your share. We are going to take in hand a ridiculous subject. Because it froths interminably. No, not interminably. Certainly, there is much to be said about it. Exactly everything that it says about itself.

Ah! If Bach or Mozart had lived long enough to set it to music for me! ... We will make up the deficiency!

Reader, after the stone,* I was bound to come to soap. It is perfectly suited to my purpose. Because it is the very type of the ridiculous subject, but one which froths interminably. It is the very symbol, the proof of my genius. You will judge by this what I might have said about the whale (for ex.) if Mr Melville, in many words no doubt, yet carelessly, had not botched this subject.

Interminably? Not so. There is, certainly, much to be said about soap. But exactly that which it says about itself until total dissolution. That is the end, thank God.

It is true that after it has disappeared, the water remains troubled for a good while, bubbles bursting, the author's hands puffy. But very clean.

Very good. This is what is perfectly suited to my purpose. It is enough.

And what could already be enough.

* Translator's note; 'The Stone,' the last piece in *The Parti Pris of Things* (1942).

Have you heard tell of the adequation of the content to the form?

*

Philosophers, you have understood me. Go lie down. In the doghouse. Back to your attic. Turn over in your sordid beds.

Here, tout n'est qu'ordre et beauté: everything shines. As one has made one's bed, so one lies down in it. And I would be angry with myself for showing anything but what I am able to put in order, to polish, adorn and open (for it is beautiful *outside*) to the beams of that smiling sensuousness.

*

Coligny, August 8th, 1946

It was also because we were, *then*, cruelly, unthinkably, absurdly deprived of soap (as we were, at the same time, of several essential things: bread, coal, potatoes), that I loved it, appreciated it, savoured it as though posthumously in my memory, and hoped to recreate it in poetry ...

À la recherche du Savon Perdu ...

Also, I often said to myself: Think now! In the *Other World* (if there is one), when we shall have sufficiently enjoyed the angels' music, what are the objects of the earth that we will remember with joy and tenderness, what are those that it would please us to evoke for our best friends among the angels, so as to make them understand their beauty, their virtues? ... As being representative of our world, our world below, and of ourselves, as being impregnated by us, our material and, perhaps, our familiar portrait? ...

Well, certainly soap is one of them!

THE EXERCISE OF SOAP

And here at last, dear listeners, is the text I ended with, between the 15th and 30th of August 1946 – and may I ask your announcer to kindly declaim here, a little as THE POET *would have done while washing his hands in the proscenium, during the play which for a moment – do you remember? – I thought of.*

But first:

HE TAKES THE NEW, WHOLE, HARD, HOMOGENEOUS, COMPACT CAKE OF SOAP OUT OF ITS PAPER WRAPPER, *and he recites:*

LET'S CRUMPLE

TO BEGIN

AS IS YOUR RIGHT DEAR READER
TO DEMAND

BY BREAKING IN OUR WAY
SOMETHING MORE THAN SILENCE

WITH ONE HAND THEN THROW AWAY
EVERY NOTE OR ROUGH DRAFT
IMPRINTED WITH ORDINARY BAD TASTE
ON THE WRAPPERS OF
THE OBJECT
SO THAT HERE WE ARE QUITE NAKED
SINCE IT HAS COME UP

IN THE OTHER
HAND
HOLDING
FOR OUR INTELLECTUAL TOILET

A LITTLE PIECE OF SOAP

PRELUDE

Well handled, we guarantee it is enough, where torrents of simple water would clean nothing, nor silence, nor your suicide in the darkest source, o absolute reader. Living under the pump is good for nothing except hiccups, unless one has in one's hand this ridiculous pebble, this ridiculous object. And the triumph of the absurd, in this matter, is it not to stand waist-deep, arms folded, in water that flees towards the Dead Sea? Believe me, the smallest washbowl would be better ... But look at him, now, under the faucet gushing with impatience to loosen the dry tongue of the soap.

Nevertheless, we must first soap our hands, and not anticipate.

DRY SOAP BEFORE USE

To take it in its saucer, the simplest, sometimes the most damaged in the house, at first it will say nothing to you, the amorphous, stubborn egg, the pebble or mediocre quoit, at which only your nose is surprised, to find it a little more strongly scented, a little more strangely also, than a stone by the fatigue of flowers.

It will say nothing to you ...

It is up to me, in fact, while it reserves itself for the festivities at hand, to talk to you about the taciturn state of our object.

And should I only talk about it briefly, with the pretext that it concerns a state of taciturnity? No, because then there would be no reason to talk about it at all. No, not if we are to repay it for its long patience between periods of use.

But how will I talk about it, then? Not loquaciously, of course, as it is not yet time for such festivities. But simply, after having detached it with difficulty from its saucer, to turn it over in our hands. Nevertheless, the kind of hardness it proposes to us already justifies, perhaps, a less rigorous way of speaking, less abrupt. Yet it will still be necessary that each phrase, based on a concrete expression of its reality, be valid for it alone, mean nothing in regard to any other object.

Finally, that one always be aware of it as being in hand, i.e. that its perfume, say, more or less vulgar, persist until the end of the discourse, and not leave this hand while it is writing, that it continually reach as far as you, dear Reader.

But isn't this too much talk to say nothing? Doubtless it needed to be turned over in our hands several more times, while saying nothing as yet itself ...

Yet impregnated as we already are, not only with its smell but with other qualities (and even with certain tiny particles of its substance) which it brings to the hands when touched, we may soon be in a position to state (even before appreciating or understanding) the serious, profound reasons for its behaviour.

Let's say that the particular kind of hardness (slightly malleable) and silence (like a verbal reserve), finally the sort of taciturnity it proposes to us, seem to us to be the sign of a dramatic inner conflict. In other words, that its appearance reveals a painfully achieved compromise – and, it seems, constantly regained as it is constantly lost again – between the temptation to endure, to conserve itself, to perpetuate itself, even, in an ever more perfect silence and dryness (the finished type of this perfection represented, if you like, by the stone) – and the feeling, on the other hand, that this is neither its duty nor, considered and honestly judged, its nature, its real end, which is rather that it be used, at the same time, of course, as it rejoices, enjoys, – to be used, I say, and to lose itself in its function, its service, and finally, to fulfil its usefulness.

For soap is meant to be a useful object, and is unable and unwilling to forget its duty. It is, at each minute, – in its very silence – capable of words and like a face about to speak.

Yes! Let us examine it and we will be touched to see, on its face, the signs of this dramatic compromise. While its inaction hardens it, conserves it, its passion for water gives it a dry tongue. Its forehead darkens, wrinkles. The anxiety of inaction cracks it. And certainly, it never conserves itself better than when it's inactive, forgotten. Yet it is bound, at the same time, to conserve all its parts in all their qualities. Also, it protects itself with no differentiated tegument, it forms no crust, shell, bark, or skin, and only reluctantly does it share in this dryness that is its health, neither dedicating nor sacrificing entirely to it any of its parts, which then would no longer be good for anything. For, although it has one and is quite aware of it, it does not have to protect in itself the delicate mechanism of an existence or an autonomous principle – without other use or justification than the conservation and perpetuation of this existence, this principle, that is to say its way of occupying and dividing Time. It has nothing to maintain save a complex of qualities or, rather, well-defined faculties proper to its function: it has only to remain adequate to its use – and there, certainly, is a lesson.

Nor does it modify in any way its form. No exterior defences. No hedgehogs, no spikes. No forward works. Neither in its form, nor in any of the essential qualities of its substance, does its silence, its solitude, its will to endure by not speaking result in any real (definitive) change. No, it remains homogenous and is completely intact – a single block – as it simply contracts, gathers itself, summons its parts to its centre.

Yet, at the same time, it can do no more than remain amenable, attractive, supple, polite. And of these qualities it can only hold the reins, shorter and shorter, during inaction. This is all that it can do. Thus showing (willy-nilly) that it doesn't so much fear a new service, a new summons, or mobilization, as it awaits it, prepares itself for it, desires to be easily picked up again, to give an amenable, polite welcome to it, in no way harsh. It is in this way also that it gathers itself for its subsequent fantastic leaps.

All this is due to the oil of which it is made and which is the basis of its qualities. What to do with it? It can't evaporate it: this is not at all in the oil's nature. It can only parcel it out in smaller and smaller vials. In more and more vials, with less oil in each. As when one arranges, in one's medicine cabinet, the bottles tightly ranged in rows. All perfectly stored in the form of an egg or quoit easy to grasp and not unpleasant to touch, although weighing a bit too lightly, perhaps, in the hand (and may you not want to throw it away, but rather chafe it, make it *give up,* evince other qualities in place of weight).

And let's say that in composing and playing this so complex and difficult role, well, that it succeeds perfectly. As soon as it has been returned to its saucer, it sets about not merely contracting, so as to maintain a maximum power to serve again, but contracting in exactly that form in which its last service left it, because it assumes that this is the form in which it will most easily be mobilized again, which will make for the most pleasure and convenience in handling again.

Thus soap appears now in its true light, in relation to the stone. Solid, serious, austere, slightly yet tenaciously scented, it certainly experiences the temptation of turning into that stone, which may appear to it as its perfect state. But it is not at all permitted to achieve this. For it is made of oil, the basis of its qualities. Soap is a useful object. It has its qualities. It has its inner conflict, for it never forgets its duty, its destiny.

Here, then, is a very sensitive individual. As sensitive to the dryness that wrinkles and cracks its forehead, as to the water whose effects on it we shall soon see.

And surely it is magnificent, given its faults, vices and weaknesses, and despite its practical qualities unknown to the stone which, however slightly, may be likened to it because of the bearing, the reserve, the discretion, the patience, the dignity, and the incorruptibility in air which it displays. Also, wouldn't it be just systematically to oppose them, commending the Cornelian severity of the stone, and dealing with soap as a facile pebble, servile, soft, domestic and not weighing much. All the better to take account of the practical qualities we have noted in it, which are unknown to the stone: this sociability, usefulness, amiability in the hand, this faithful and persistent adequation to what is expected of it. For all that, it is nearly as incorruptible in air and, kept dry, I don't think it would yield to anything in longevity ...

Certainly, it seems to me that this is to its honour. But I must now deal with

THE SPONTANEOUS CONFUSION OF SOAP IN TRANQUIL WATER

For in water, it will be objected, what inferiority! It melts before the eye, vanishes almost at once. In this surrounding, in fact, it seems to prove its obvious inferiority ... Nevertheless, let's look more closely.

Here again, I don't think that pejorative expressions can be advanced with any justice or reason. To be frank, I laugh, on the contrary, in advance, at your confusion – when you will attentively observe the confusion of the soap itself with the liquid, – because then you will feel your own inferiority in the air of time and the serum of eternal causes. And perhaps you can already guess the use I will make of this, the brilliant piece of bravado during which, getting down at last to the proper function of soap, I will astonish you with the evidence of its, of my genius, and of the truth that it conveys. All the criticisms at the end of your tongue on the triviality of this subject, its affectedness, my banal way of dealing with it will be laughably disconcerted, will suddenly find themselves mocked by waves of dazzling light. But it is not yet time for this.

Let us observe, then, the soap's behaviour at the bottom of a quantity of water when, forgetfully and inadvertently, its owner has left it there for the time being. Let us immediately note that it does not last well there, that it is diminished almost at once. But we should also, at almost the same time, note that even there it gives proof of a sufficiently peculiar dignity.

Rather than let itself be rolled about by water, like pebbles, the natural stones, it prefers to instantly melt into it. And why, in fact, should it consent to pass its life in being unilaterally caressed by the waves. When it knows, is aware that it's part of a *ménage à trois*, a trio, and does not play its part willingly, with brio, except in these conditions?

So much so that in a tête-à-tête with water, it does not interest itself in the question, lets itself be diminished with a perfect passivity, does not lend itself in the least to any game of friendly jostling, jolting, pokes.

Rather, it clings to the bottom and – how should I say it? – I won't say that it gives up the ghost, because it is its whole body that it lets disperse in trailing fumes, in fuliginous trails, slow in their movement and disappearance. Its whole body gives up the ghost in fumes that are slow to dissipate. Or rather, it gives up its body at the same time as its soul, and, when it breathes its last, at the same time the last trace of its body has disappeared.

Far, then, from letting itself be caressed by water, it prefers to melt into it, I have just said how. And I don't think that anyone in the world should remain indifferent to this. There is no reason to mistake it. The fact is, besides, that water, the original guilty one, soon learns the consequences. There it is, deeply troubled, in a relatively considerable amount. It has lost face and we see it deprived of the marvellous limpidity, the interior lucidity that is the usual reward of its clear conscience. Above all, the usual reward, if one considers it coldly, of its habit of usually banishing to its depths or its surface the bodies that come to visit it; this is due to a unique density that protects enormous quantities of liquid.

Thus towards stones, say, water behaves with a sort of indifference or flippancy. Certainly it uses them up in the end, yet is not changed by them in any way. Its eyes remain as clear, as cold; it lets the particles or debris that it detaches or conquers from its victim drop immediately to its depths. It instantly decants itself. Certainly, the war of water with stone is infinitely longer than with soap, but more difficult ... can one say so? The water wages it carelessly, without interest or worrying about it, as if mechanically. It has many other things to do, performs many other duties at the same time: it simultaneously carries on many other activities, other occupations; imperturbably. It cannot be beaten in this war, or seriously bothered, and never gives the impression that it is. It is always, at each minute – though very slowly – victorious.

It is very difficult for it, however, to rid itself of soap, and the traces of its crime. The soap avenges itself for the humiliation it undergoes by intimately blending with the water, marrying itself to it in the most apparent way. This egg, this flat dab, this little almond quickly grows into a Chinese fish, with its veils, its kimonos and wide sleeves, and thus celebrates its marriage with water. It is then, during an impressively staged ceremony, that its confusion with water takes place, and the disappearance of its form into memory. (At the same time, all memory of dirtiness dissolves.) As for the water, it remains deeply troubled, moved. An enormous amount of it has, as I've said, lost face. It finds itself seriously punished for it. It will not succeed in ridding itself of the soap, and of the traces of its crime, except by a considerable afflux of reinforcements brought up en masse, and by an agitation very significant of the emotion, the remorse it feels; except, finally, by quantity. Only by calling on its quantity. It is quantity, here, that drowns quality, makes it indistinct, proportionately (or relatively) indifferent or insignificant. Insignificant, one was already too quick to say ...

Now, let's take the soap out of the water and consider each of the two adversaries.

This one, shy, slipping away, fleeing, secret, heroic, disquietingly evasive ... leading what is called a dissipated life ... a bad boy because of its shyness and dignity. It circulates, flees, makes a thousand affected gestures, swathes itself in veils and finally prefers to dissolve, rather than let itself be caressed, unilaterally swallowed up by the water ...

It happens that we have lost it and must gropingly fish it out again, very much diminished, half melted, softened up, bags under its eyes, unrecognizable, like someone who has 'had it'. Are we to regret this? Certainly not. We find it, as I say, smaller, diminished, exhausted sometimes, thin as it can be – yet with all dignity intact ...

As for the other, an enormous amount troubled, having lost face ...

Which one is the victor?

Etc. ...

SOAPY WATER AND SOAP BUBBLES

Saturated with soap, the water froths at the least movement. Wants to join the air, climbs in the assault of the sky. Grabs the air's arm, climbs the sky's knees ... throws itself into the air's arms ... throws itself on the sky's neck ... Displays even a sort of aerostatic pretention. Displays a sort of exaltation, and even an aerostatic pretention. Sometimes achieves, in this respect, miraculous, brilliant, short-lived success.

It seems, at any rate, that its mood is made much more communicative by it. May it be communicated then! Intimately joined with soap, it will communicate it at the same time as itself.

... Yet always in a disorderly way, because always occasionally. Much more than a systematic desire, it concerns a disposition. A facility or faculty of elocution.

... We are nearly at this point. Saturated with our subject, not a word that doesn't evolve in various allusions. We have become capable of an unlimited succession of bubbles, which we release as they come to us, singly or in groups and not tampering with them: for we know that they will explode, I don't say merely at the least provocation, but at the least contact, and even at the least breath, or critical look – as also at the least exaggeration, exasperation of their inner vanity ...

It happens that, in this adventure, we have lost the piece of soap itself, and that we have to gropingly fish it out again, very much diminished, half melted, softened up, bags under its eyes, unrecognizable, like someone who has 'had it'.

Shall we regret this? – Certainly not.

Our most successful bubbles, *our only successful ones* are doubtless those that are the least worked. For can one work on a bubble? Surely not, – unless (carefully) with the very breath that gives it birth.

It is only necessary to blow it with an even enough breath, with just the right pretentiousness, a movement of the soul at once measured and persistent, yet not too much so – until it detaches itself quasi-spontaneously from the pipe.

It is presence of mind that's required, at the moment of expiration … (of *breathation*).

Those bubbles that have been overly worked burst and fall in drops of water. And what vanity to want to remake them at all! There is only one solution: to blend them again with the liquid mass, to lose them there with no regret.

… All this is much more, I think, than extended metaphors …

*

All this is much more, I think, than extended metaphors … These bubbles are beings in every (in their own) respect. Instructive in the highest degree. They rise in revolt from the earth, and take you with them. New qualities, unforeseen, until now unknown, ignored, are added to the known to constitute the perfection and particularity of a being-in-every-respect. Thus they escape being symbols. And their aspect changes. It no longer concerns an aspect of usefulness, or serviceability to man. Instead of their serving for something, it concerns a creation and no longer an explanation. There is something more in the conclusion than in the premises, because some premise was added which, mysteriously, managed to curl the sphere, completely curve it, and allowed it to detach itself and fly away.

And the feeling of happiness that their sight stirs in man is not deceptive: he is happy because he has *gained* something.

*

Here, then are some of these bubbles which besides, for the most part, are innocent and unpremeditated.

For who – except by a rather infantile and old-fashioned game – while performing his intellectual toilet, would want to take a pipe and blow literary bubbles.

No, it only concerns soap and washing one's hands, like my ancestor Pontius Pilate – of whom I am so proud that having said: 'What is truth?' – he should wash his hands of the death of the Just One (or the exalted one) and thus be the sole person in the story to enter history with clean hands, having done his duty without big gestures, big symbols, wailing and fatuity.

But after all, if I push the analysis further, it is much less a question of propelling bubbles myself, than to prepare the liquid for you (or the solution, as one so aptly says), to tempt you with a saturation blending, in which you may, after my example, exercise yourself, (satisfy yourself) indefinitely, in your turn …

RINSING

At this point, a new reflection occurs. It is necessary to end. The skin is puffy, although very clean. We have obtained what we wanted from the soap. And perhaps a little more, even.

Paragraph of fresh water. Rinsing *a*) the body *b*) the soap. It is put back in its saucer, returned to its austere oval and its power to serve again. Meanwhile the body is already engrossed with a new object: THE TURKISH TOWEL ...

*

But that is another story altogether, which I will tell you some other time ...

APPENDICES

APPENDIX I

VARIANT OF THE ADDRESS TO THE GERMAN LISTENERS

Paris. December 6th, 1964

Ladies, Young Ladies, Gentlemen,

You are now hearing, you have just this moment begun to hear the reading of the first text ever written by me for radio.

Remember this word, I ask you: first, first text.

Written, then, not to appear before your eyes, but to penetrate your mind by way of your ears.

And you will tell me that it is as if I had prepared a scholarly or other paper: a course or a lecture.

But no, for you constitute an extremely different audience: in the first place, an audience assumed to be much more numerous than any which might be gathered in a lecture hall; assumed, then, to be very numerous but also very dispersed, of indefinite aspect, of which it is perfectly impossible for me, not only to see, but even to imagine the various faces, the various ears, their conditions of listening, the attitudes in which you have congealed to hear me – and besides, some may be listening as they move about their apartment, going about their business; you may even be having some conversation or other ... and I would have to know this ... BOOM! *in order to raise my voice higher, to make you jump –* BOOM! *– , to force* *myself on your attention, to make you give me your more concentrated, more serious attention ...*

And now, I assume that I have this ...

But put yourself in my place: comment procédé-je? *

Or rather, I should say: comment est-ce que je procède?

Why should I say, est-ce que je procède?

Because, if you were reading rather than listening, I should have been able to write: procédé-je; *however, as you are listening, this form consequently seems imprecise, dubious, not distinguishable in sound from the simple past or imperfect tense of the same verb. I have, then, to prefer the form:* comment est-ce que je procède?

I will now answer this question.

Well, the truth is that I do not proceed at all by speaking the words – no, that's not true, I say them inside myself only, with the least sound leaving my lips – I proceed, in fact, with a pen in my hand, putting marks on a blank sheet of paper – and I am not more advanced than you: I am only at the beginning ... (Enough on this point.)

Ladies and Gentlemen,

When it was suggested to me that I write something for you, I had the idea, eminently selfish, of profiting from this occasion to complete a very old project, for which I had taken many notes, had tried relentlessly to give successive shapes to, had, in despair of its

* Translator's note: This is impossible to translate. Ponge is referring to the likeness in sound of *procédé-je, procédais-je,* etc. ('How do I proceed?')

premise, abandoned the dossier of in my drawers, which I have just taken out again and which is at this moment – kindly imagine it – placed on my left, on the table before which I have seated myself to write.

But attention! Wait! Listen to the noise of this dossier, which I have just lifted up and which I will, for you to hear, let fall again on my table ... (Noise.)

The title inscribed on the cover of this dossier – tied with string, backed – in my own large handwriting is as follows: Soap.

How then, Ladies and Gentlemen, can I hope, today and by speaking, to complete a work conceived in the past, abandoned a very long time ago, which was meant to be read?

And how, and why was I able to imagine this as being possible?

– Doubtless because, to deal with the first point, its matter, today, still seems to me of sufficient interest to merit its being worked on, given shape, and published; also because, not having considered it for a long time, I hope to see it objectively and to be able, in perfecting it, to bring my critical faculties to bear better than when I was in the middle of it, or, as the phrase is, when I was following my nose.

– And, for the second point, because the fact of addressing myself by speaking to persons who are dispersed and sparse like those, certainly, who read books, yet whom I imagine today and at this very minute as gathered together in the flesh, if not in space then at least in time, to hear my text without having – I speak of them – anything to do but listen – and without, myself, having to be, by their presence before my eyes (as in a lecture hall), stimulated, annoyed or inhibited, nor to risk – by their reactions which I cannot, on the present radiophonic occasion, register as they happen – deviating from the sense of my discourse – the fact, then, of addressing myself orally to a public of this sort obliges me to end in a relatively short time – I refer equally to the time in which my work is to be finished and that of its delivery, then of its length – and, on the other hand, obliges me in some manner to loosen up my language, for everything being necessarily effaced from hearing as it is said, I cannot use overly dense language (which implies its ability to be read several times, or lingered over long enough); it may even be necessary to repeat certain phrases several times, as is done in music ...

And it seems to me also that if I have chosen to offer for your hearing this particular work, the dossier of which is here before me on my table, it is because this dossier, being one of the largest and already one of the most worked on among those of mine which are not as yet completed, therefore mattered enough for me to try, by this means, to bring it to an end – as it was also to give you the fruits of a long work rather than chancily improvise for you on some other theme.

But finally, why soap then? Why have I wanted, for more than twenty years now, to undertake an exercise on this theme, a priori so trivial, so prosaic?

Well! (if I may say so) we will very clearly see why ...

APPENDIX II

I. PROEM

Paris, December 28th, 1964

Certainly I owe much to my laziness. By my laziness I mean that exercised (now and in the past) towards what I *should not* do.

I have often said that man – that is to say 'one', that is to say 'me', – has had in our time a great desire 'to change'. Not so much, to be truthful, to change in his 'being', as in what he chose to be *with it,* what to show of it, do with it.

It is not so much, in fact, novelty that I seek, as distinction, authenticity.

For myself, then, treatises or works of art based on human psychology (or morality) have never seemed to me to be *my thing*. I mean works of morality or psychology *as such*.

After all, it *had been* done; done by others; and that it was done as well as it could be, I have never doubted.

Each time that I re-read the masters, the modern as well as the ancient ones, I was seized with enthusiasm and admiration, yet at the same time I exclaimed inside myself: 'Done!' (and so, not to be done again).

On one hand, in fact, the models (of minds, characters and mores) proposed by these works seemed to me *beyond reach,* in every sense of this expression, a little like the gods or heroes of ancient ritual; on the other hand, I experienced a violent need to bend down to the earth, to drink water, to finger dirt, to pick fruits, to physically encounter things. This alone seemed to me natural and worth my work: it being understood that I certainly expected to find in them the principles of mind and morality, yet such as would, at least, be slightly unusual, in which I would recognize myself and which it would be my task to raise to the dignity of future heroes, gods, thrones and dominations, without too much deceiving myself, meanwhile, as to their absolute 'truth', at once establishing and abolishing them through the virtues of a new *Scripture*.

And this is the wherefore of *things* (and, for example, soap) in my book, ma bible (in *mon bible*, I would like to write).

II. NEW LABOURS FOR SOAP

Paris, December 29th, 1964

Ballets of veils, of floating sashes, whirling, eddying, falling back, self-enfolding, self-unfolding: it was what we called, when I was young, ballets *à la Loïe Fuller*.

Ballets of tulle, of bubbles, of froth, of foam, ballets of rage and ecstasy; ballets of irritation and exultation, of flocculation, of volubility.

Ballets of emulsion and evaporization, of gauze and gasification; ballets of dissolution.

Ballets of explosion, slow explosions in extreme slow motion, not in rectilinear bursts, but rather like large curvilinear ribbons.

Yes, a sort of very slow deflagrations, in curved lines, or volubilines.

And aren't cakes of soap like hand grenades, bursting in a very slow way on trajectories like curvilinear ribbons?

It concerns defeats, of course, much more than victories, but especially frothy ones, ravished, full of delectation, mouth-waterings, envelopments and developments, excessive – and finally purificatory.

A way of giving up yet occupying space, a very particular way. Of a diminution and exhaustion of the central core, which gives itself the air of a recrudescence (ah! this is excellent, to say '*which gives itself the air*', as it exactly expresses the emulsion).

Finally, it concerns, here, one of the secrets of nature ... And I ask myself now, wasn't there, when I began this study, some reminiscence, very much worked towards its abstraction in my memory, of the *exodus* of 1940, as I had undergone it a few years before ... ?

APPENDIX III

DIE SEIFE, SOAP: THE WORDS, THE THING

Paris, January 1st, 1965

Ladies and Gentlemen,

Die Seife, die Seifenkugel*: you know what it is, you are well acquainted with this thing, or matter, this sort of compound of fatty matters (consequently not soluble in water) and caustic alkaline salts* (*καυστικὸς, καιειν, to burn) which possesses detergent qualities and which is used to wash and whiten all things and, notably, your linen and your very skin.*

Pliny lets it be understood that it is a Gallic invention: 'Galliarum hoc inventum', he says (XXXIII, 12, 51).

The Greek words σάπων – from which are surely derived the Latin sapo, *the French* savon, *the English* soap *and, it may be, although this seems less evident, your German* Seife *as well – will also have been of gallic provenance (Celtic).*

The thing that this word designates, of extremely common usage in our regions for, therefore, *two or three millennia, occurs in the form of pieces, stones, leaves and balls of variable designs and qualities; sometimes in pastes, pomades, unguents. It is remarkably soluble in water but, as with all viscous liquids, when they are stirred or struck or poured from a height, the air bubbles which are in combination with the water, not being able to break their enve-*

lopes, prevail so that it rises, in the form of foam, or froth.

This enhances greatly the operation of washing and whitening for which it is employed. It also renders, in a way, this operation joyous. And how can one fail to notice that the joy in question is fully realized by one's certainty of being easily able to put an end to it, by the sudden, violent addition of an extra amount of water! When it concerns linen, a glorious flag is soon hung out – and, in any case, whether it concerns linen or teeth or skin, or even dishes or an automobile, what pride, what good conscience, what joy!

As for the words and images that will have been able adequately to render this, isn't it evident that they will be the accepted signs and modes of pure exultation itself …

Isn't this worth the trouble of working on?

APPENDIX IV

OBJECTS OF HUMAN MAKING* IN GENERAL; CERTAIN KEYS AND CIPHERS IN PARTICULAR

Paris, January 2nd, 1965

With regard to the commonest objects of human making, the simplest or most elementary in appearance, the most indispensable also – or which seem so to us –, we have become, ourselves, we 'civilized' men, in comparison to our distant (not so distant) ancestors, very different; very other, in fact.

We have come to consider these objects as natural objects, as objects which are due to us from nature without the least effort on our part, unless that of paying for them (not much). And who would be unable to buy, for example, a piece of soap?

When, through extraordinary circumstances, it happens that we lack such objects, having become 'unfindable', we are seized with a sharp feeling of surprise and frustration which, in a way, unbalances us. Morally (that is: practically), we find ourselves obliged to make a choice. We may decide to learn either to do without them, or to make them ourselves starting from nothing, which is in fact to say from the first things that come to hand. At any rate, we

* Translator's note: I am sorry to have lost a fruitful pun here. Ponge's word is *fabrication*, which in French has only the right tinge of the pejorative. An analogous English word would be 'forging'.

find ourselves, with regard to them, disabused: we finally see them, instead of purely and simply utilizing them.

Their precious character appears to us then, their value is revealed, At the same time, our own value in our own eyes changes: we weigh it in relation to them. The world becomes interesting again, as a game does when it's 'serious', as one says: you know, when one decides to be an *interested party,* so that the game is no longer 'for fun' but 'for real', 'for money'. Some passion (the taste for risk or, in short, that of drama) then comes into play. The rhythm of the blood accelerates; nervous activity and expenditure increase.

Let us now consider the poets, the artists. Let us consider them within the society which surrounds them, and try to discover what distinguishes them from it. So, for example, it will happen that a painter *sees* a still-life (a kitchen table, say) in its *value,* in the sense which, in the preceding analysis, I have arrived at for this idea, this word. Again, for example, a poet will happen to envisage in this way any object: bread, a candle, a piece of meat, a piece of soap.

It is generally thought that artists, being accustomed to – and, in a sense, the *subjects* of – this way of seeing, that is to say, temperamentally out of kilter in a facile, automatic, usual, common world, that artists thereby show, well, what? if not their disequilibrium, their madness or, at least, their inconceivable naivety.

Possible! Possible!

Nevertheless, doesn't this seem to you, on the contrary, I mean: after our little analysis just now, as something positive, rather, as the sign of a capacity, a supplementary faculty, perhaps, as a sign of superiority? (I simply ask the question.)

I will be told, of course, that artists, seeing things and causing them to be seen in this way, remain at the stage of undeception and in no manner pass this phase, do not arrive at the act of readaptation, of aseity, or of making.

Indeed! Indeed! (Even so, if only temporarily, I grant it.) They may at least be considered, already, as useful initiators in a certain 'reality' of the world, which may well become, at times, more difficult, more interesting, more exciting than it ordinarily seems. Finally, as trainers (in the sense of sports-training), as gym-teachers, guides, hospital attendants, who knows? or, roughly speaking, as moralists.

This is, perhaps, the utility of poets and artists. But let us now consider the pleasure they procure.

Well then, this pleasure usually stems from the fact that they know how to hide, to dissimulate their usefulness, that they do not turn into professors or moralists. That they limit themselves to transmitting to you their own emotion, their surprise, their wonder, their sense of the unexpected, the fatal, even of the tragic in daily reality. That they do not propose for you to change it, but only to see it – and this, in the same conditions of quiet, security, tranquillity, comfort, equilibrium – evidently factitious – which you are enjoying then, at the same time.

This is to say that it really seems to be a question of a game, of an activity of leisure in the midst of daily automatic life, to which you may return at any minute. Of a game without importance, or so it seems, and, as one says, for free.

And it need hardly be said that the extreme form of this game is poetry, the purely verbal game, with no imitation or representation of 'life' itself; not, then, the novel, history, or drama, but the poem. I mean here not the sentimental, subjective poem, but the eulogy or willed poem which is, besides, the most structured, the most disengaged, the most transposed, the 'coldest' possible.

There is, here, an utterness, a gratuitous object, at once natural and precious, precise as it can be and, by this very fact, mysterious. 'Gratuitous', the value of which will not appear until the wished moment, that is to say the endured (dramatic) moment, I mean to say at the moment of a true 'reading'.

We are put into possession of a very precious set of tools, which look as if they were good for nothing, but which will prove, at times, to be inconceivably useful.

In short, a 'standard' or universal set of tools. And finally, it may be, a sort of universal *key* or *cipher*.

Now, be so kind (after having 'caught your breath' a minute) as to read again from its beginning the long text which precedes this – not without having, previously, persuaded yourself of the following: namely that the commonest, most indispensable objects of human making, which are due to us from nature (so it seems to us), but which we may lack, etc., etc., those which one ordinarily utilizes without any thought for them, as Monsieur Jourdain used to do with prose, include – as well as bread, soap, or electricity – words and figures of speech: it will immediately be seen that the real *makers* (and not merely contemplators) of these objects are the writers, the poets – and that it is on us, and on us alone, as such, that the power has devolved to forge the keys of the world, or the ciphers which allow us to recognize ourselves in it, and to open or close its doors at (... if you believe in this word ...) 'liberty'.

APPENDIX V

RUBBING ONE'S HANDS. WITH SOMETHING. WRITING AND READING. INTRODUCTION TO THE MORALITY OF THE OBJOY. END OF THE BOOK.

Paris, January 3rd, 1965

Why then is rubbing one's hands, in our regions, an accepted sign of inner satisfaction, and even exultation?

Be sure, we will be able to formulate some more or less plausible explanations of this.

Already, in regard to *plausible,* how can one fail to connect the act of rubbing hands with that of applause, in which two hands, one against the other, are also employed: clapping rather than rubbing, it's true – and consequently producing a supplementary acoustic phenomenon: a noise. Here the satisfaction expressed is no longer meant for oneself, but for some other person, whom one wishes to hear it clearly and publicly.

But let's get back to rubbing hands. Couldn't it be taken as the sign in petto of a sort of 'linking up', satisfying in itself, of corporal identity, comparable to that attempted by the dog when it tries to bite its tail; be noted then, correlatively to this hypothesis, that among the many double, symmetrical organs in the human body (and in most other physical bodies, whatever they may be), hands are among the rare ones which are easily able to come together?

Very natural, therefore, that they should not abstain from doing so – and congratulating each other ...

As for the rubbing, would not this be, then, a redoubling, a multiplication of simple seizing, just as a caress, for example, must be repeated, be made insistent for it to produce its full effect, ending finally in some nervous modification, I mean to say some spasm or orgasm.

The production of its own sign thus becoming the condition of accomplishment of whatever it may be ... Yes! Yes! It is in exactly this way that writing must be thought of: not as the transcription, according to conventional rules, of some idea (exterior or anterior) but, in reality, as an orgasm: as the orgasm of a being or structure, let's say, conventional to begin with, of course – yet which must fulfil itself, give itself, exultantly, as such: in a word, to signify itself.

Let us now return to Soap, that is to rubbing our hands *with* something and, so to speak, by means of a means.

This is done, no longer (as in applause or the rubbing of hands) as a consequence or sign of an achieved result, but for a result to be attained: a washing or whitening, as it happens.

To give this *means* its full importance, so as to make it yield its maximum output, to obtain from it its utmost favours (a continual gift of saliva, for example): this truly is the game. the verbal exercise par excellence; this is 'poetry'; this is very 'morality'.

And it will have been necessary, of course, at this point in our reflections, to put our arm around the waist of the *with* idea, that is to say, the word itself.

What then is this *with* (*avec*) if not *av-vec, apud hoc*: near to, in the company of.

Would this not, then, be its entry in society, its being accompanied by some other (creature or thing), by some object, finally, which would allow whoever it might be to realize his personal identity, to disengage it from what it is not, to clean it, to decarbonize it? To signify *oneself*? To perpetuate oneself, finally, in the objoy.

Our *paradise,* in short: will it not have been *the others*?

*

As for the paradise of this book, what is it? What else could it be, if not, reader, *your reading it* (how it does bite its tail in these last lines).

*

So here this book is linked up; our top set spinning our SOAP in orbit.

(And all the *stages* or successive chapters fired for its launching may well, already, have re-entered the *atmosphere,* the platitude of oblivion, as it was that of the project.)

Its fate now depends only on the material nature of which these signs and their support are part.

END OF THE BOOK

THE AUTHOR

Francis Ponge was born at Montpellier on March 27th, 1899, of aristocratic Protestant stock. His early childhood was spent in Avignon; his lycée years in Caen and Paris. Music, Latin authors and Philosophy appear to have been his guiding interests. At fourteen, he travelled in the Low Countries and in Britain. After University studies in Paris and Strasbourg, marked by a crippling inability to pass oral examinations and interrupted by a brief but influential army recruitment at the end of the First World War, Ponge began to make himself known in French literary circles: the *Nouvelle Revue Française* and the Surrealists. But he disliked movements and regular work (there were brief stays at the N.R.F. and with Hachette) and his membership of the Communist Party from 1936 to 1946 was a modest one. During the Second World War he was soldier, insurance worker and Resistance organizer. From 1947 to 1951 were the lean years, interrupted by a trip to Algeria in 1947–8 with Henri Calet and Michel Leiris. In 1952 he began to teach for the Alliance Française. His fame began to grow with the N.R.F. homage in 1956, the respect shown for him by the avant-garde magazine *Tel Quel* in its first number and the exhibition of his works at the Bibliothèque Doucet in 1960.

SELECTED BIBLIOGRAPHY

A list of the principal works of Francis Ponge with the dates of their first appearance

DOUZE PETITS ÉCRITS (Gallimard, Paris, 1926)
LE PARTI PRIS DES CHOSES (Gallimard, Paris, 1942)
LA GUÊPE (Seghers, Paris, 1945)
L'ŒILLET, LA GUÊPE, LE MIMOSA (Mermod, Lausanne, 1946)
BRAQUE LE RÉCONCILIATEUR (Skira, Geneva, 1946)
LE CARNET DU BOIS DE PINS (Mermod, Lausanne, 1947)
PROÊMES (Gallimard, Paris, 1948)
LE PEINTRE À L'ÉTUDE (Gallimard, Paris, 1948)
MY CREATIVE METHOD (Atlantis, Zurich, 1949)
LA SEINE (La Guilde du Livre, Lausanne, 1950)
LA RAGE DE L'EXPRESSION (Mermod, Lausanne, 1952)
LE GRAND RECUEIL: I. Lyres; II. Méthodes; III. Pièces (Gallimard, Paris, 1961)
TOME PREMIER (Gallimard, Paris, 1965)
POUR UN MALHERBE (Gallimard, Paris, 1965)
LE SAVON (Gallimard, Paris, 1967)
NOUVEAU RECUEIL (Gallimard, Paris, 1967)

N.B.: The last five items amount to a 'Collected Works'. A great many of Ponge's works were first issued in highly limited de luxe editions. A list of these can be found in Philippe Sollers's *Francis Ponge* (Coll. Poètes d'Aujourd'hui, no. 95; Seghers, Paris, 1963)

CAPE EDITIONS

1 The Scope of Anthropology, Claude Lévi-Strauss
2 Call Me Ishmael, Charles Olson
3 Writing Degree Zero, Roland Barthes
4 Elements of Semiology, Roland Barthes
5 I Wanted to Write a Poem, William Carlos Williams
6 The Memorandum, Václav Havel
7 Selected Poems, Nazim Hikmet
9 Tango, Slawomir Mrozek
10 On Love ... Aspects of a Single Theme, José Ortega y Gasset
11 Manhood, Michel Leiris
12 Bees: Their Vision, Chemical Senses, and Language, Karl von Frisch
13 Lunar Caustic, Malcolm Lowry
14 Twenty Prose Poems, Charles Baudelaire
15 Journeys, Günter Eich
16 A Close Watch on the Trains, Bohumil Hrabal
17 Mayan Letters, Charles Olson
18 The Courtship Habits of the Great Crested Grebe, Julian Huxley
19 The Supermale, Alfred Jarry
20 Poems & Antipoems, Nicanor Parra
21 In Praise of Krishna: Songs from the Bengali
22 History Will Absolve Me, Fidel Castro
23 Selected Poems, Georg Trakl
24 Selected Poems, Yves Bonnefoy
25 Ferdinand, Louis Zukofsky
26 The Recluse, Adalbert Stifter
27 Dialectical Materialism, Henri Lefebvre
29 Soul on Ice, Eldridge Cleaver
30 The Human Sciences and Philosophy, Lucien Goldmann
31 Selected Poems, André Breton